S0-AWW-670

- The Colonies -

The
North Carolina
Colony

Tamara L. Britton

ABDO Publishing Company

visit us at
www.abdopub.com

Published by ABDO Publishing Company, 4940 Viking Drive, Edina, Minnesota 55435.
Copyright © 2001 by Abdo Consulting Group, Inc. International copyrights reserved in all
countries. No part of this book may be reproduced in any form without written permission from
the publisher.

Printed in the United States.

Cover Photo Credit: North Wind Picture Archives
Interior Photo Credits: North Wind Picture Archives (pages 9, 11, 13, 15, 17, 19, 21, 23, 25, 27,
   29); Corbis (page 7)

Contributing Editors: Bob Italia, Kate A. Furlong, and Christine Fournier
Book Design and Graphics: Neil Klinepier

Library of Congress Cataloging-in-Publication Data

Britton, Tamara L., 1963-
   The North Carolina Colony / Tamara L. Britton.
      p. cm. -- (The colonies)
   Includes index.
   ISBN 1-57765-582-6
   1. North Carolina--History--Colonial period, ca. 1600-1775--Juvenile literature. [1.
North Carolina--History--Colonial period, ca. 1600-1775.] I. Title. II. Series.

2001022778

Contents

The North Carolina Colony

Native Americans first settled North Carolina's land. The most powerful tribe was the Cherokee. They lived in the mountains.

In 1524, the first European explorers came to North Carolina. They wanted to settle there and make money from the land. But none of their colonies were successful.

In the 1650s, English colonists from Virginia Colony moved to present-day North Carolina. In 1663, England's King Charles I gave North Carolina's land to eight Englishmen. They ruled over the land until 1729. During this time, people came to the colony from many different countries.

In the late 1700s, England's king made the colonists pay high taxes. The colonists disliked the taxes. This led to the **American Revolution**.

The colonists won the war. They created the United States of America. North Carolina became the new nation's twelfth state.

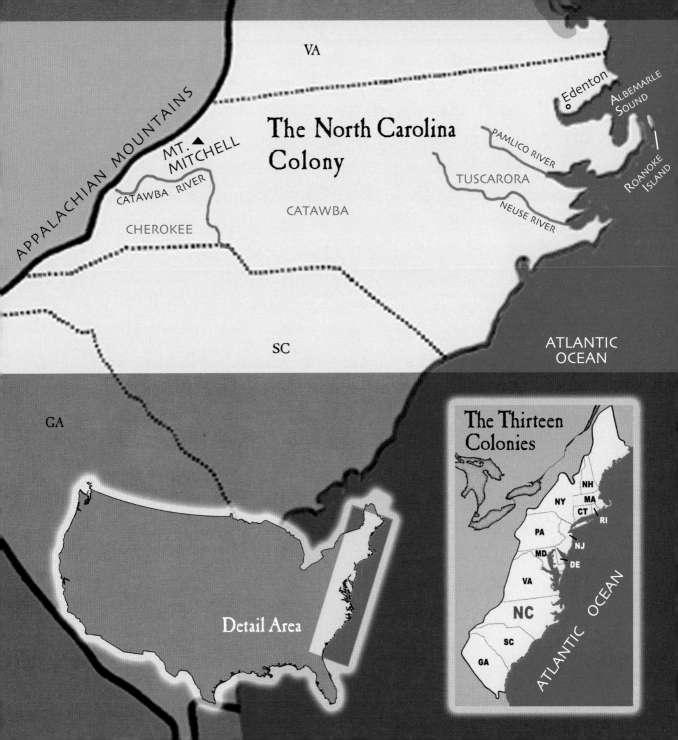

VA

APPALACHIAN MOUNTAINS

MT. MITCHELL

The North Carolina Colony

Edenton

ALBEMARLE SOUND

PAMLICO RIVER

TUSCARORA

ROANOKE ISLAND

CATAWBA RIVER

CATAWBA

CHEROKEE

NEUSE RIVER

SC

ATLANTIC OCEAN

GA

Detail Area

The Thirteen Colonies

NH
NY
MA
CT
RI
PA
NJ
MD
DE
VA
NC
SC
GA

ATLANTIC OCEAN

Early History

North Carolina is a state on the mid-Atlantic coastline. The Appalachian (ap-uh-LAY-shun) Mountains are in the west. The central part of the state is a **piedmont** region. It leads to a low, coastal plain in the east. Many rivers run from the mountains into the Atlantic Ocean.

The coastal plain has many swamps and lakes. Its soil is good for growing crops. The piedmont region has rocky, claylike soil. The Appalachian Mountains are the highest land in North Carolina. Mount Mitchell is 6,684 feet (2039 m) high. It is the highest point east of the Mississippi River.

Before the Europeans came, Native Americans called North Carolina home. The largest Native American group was the Cherokee. Smaller groups, like the Tuscarora (tus-cuh-ROR-uh) and Catawba (kuh-TAOW-buh), lived in North Carolina as well.

The Cherokee lived in homes made of timber frames covered with bark or wood and coated with clay. They built their homes in the mountains of western North Carolina. The Catawba lived along the Catawba River. The Tuscarora lived between the Neuse and Pamlico Rivers.

North Carolina's mountainous landscape

The First Explorers

Explorer Giovanni da Verrazzano (gee-oh-VAH-nee dah ver-rah-ZAH-noh) sailed past North Carolina in 1524. He was the first European to explore the area. He was working for France's King Francis I. Verrazzano's party mapped the land around Cape Hatteras.

In the 1520s, Lucas Vásques de Ayllón (LOO-kass VAS-kays day eye-YON) of Spain sent people to explore North Carolina. In 1526, he sailed up the Cape Fear River with six ships full of colonists. That July, they tried to start a Spanish colony there. But many of the colonists died from illness or hunger. In October, the remaining colonists left.

Hernando de Soto explored North Carolina for Spain in 1540. He was searching for gold. In 1562, the French tried to start a colony in North Carolina. But the colony failed.

Then England's Queen Elizabeth I gave Sir Walter Raleigh permission to start a colony. In 1585, he sent seven ships to North Carolina's Roanoke Island. At this time, North Carolina and Roanoke Island were part of the land called Virginia.

The colonists settled on Roanoke Island. But they soon ran out of food. So in June 1586, the colonists returned to England.

In May 1587, Raleigh sent more colonists to Roanoke Island. The ship's captain left the colonists on the island. Then he went back to England to get more supplies. In 1590, he returned. But the colonists had disappeared. This settlement is called the Lost Colony of Roanoke.

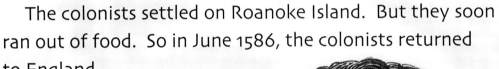
Giovanni da Verrazzano

First Settlements

In 1629, England's King Charles I granted a **charter** to Robert Heath. The charter gave him North Carolina's land. It called the land Carolana. But Heath never made use of his land.

During the 1650s, colonists moved south into North Carolina's land at various times. So North Carolina has no record of its first settlement.

In October 1662, the Virginia Colony's government recognized the colonists in the North Carolina area. They called it the Southern Plantation, and named Samuel Stephens its commander. Stephens appointed a sheriff who collected taxes and kept order.

In 1663, King Charles II decided to take control of the land. He renamed the land Carolina. He owed money to eight men. They had helped him become king. So he gave them a charter for Carolina's land. The eight men were called **proprietors**. They received the land from Albemarle Sound south to the Florida border.

The **proprietors** encouraged people to come to Carolina. People came from New England, Barbados, and Virginia. Soon the people in the Albemarle region began to form a community.

England's King Charles I and the signatures of the proprietors

Colonial Government

As people settled in Carolina, the **proprietors** created Albemarle County. They chose a governor, a council, a secretary, and a **surveyor** for the county. The **freemen** of the county elected an assembly to represent them.

In 1664, William Drummond became Albemarle County's first governor. He established courts, pardoned offenders, and collected taxes. He formed a **militia** (muh-LISH-uh) and gave land grants. He also conducted business with other colonies and the Native Americans.

For many years, Carolina's government was unstable. Many of the appointed governors were dishonest. So in 1691, the proprietors named Philip Ludwell governor for all of Carolina. Ludwell brought peace to the colony.

Carolina soon began to grow. It was difficult for one governor to control all of the people. So in 1712, the proprietors separated North Carolina from South Carolina. They appointed Edward Hyde North Carolina's new governor.

In 1715, colonists passed a law that required towns of more than 60 families to be represented in the colony's assembly. In 1722, Edenton became the seat of the colony's government.

In 1729, King George II bought North Carolina Colony's land from seven of the **proprietors**. Then, North Carolina was a royal colony.

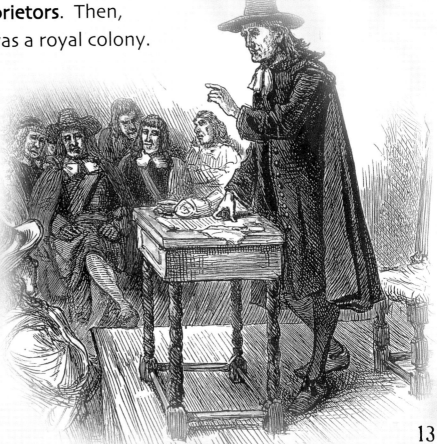

North Carolina governor John Archdale addresses the assembly.

13

Life in the Colony

North Carolinians were divided into social classes. The upper-class people were priests, public officials, or planters. A few were educated at Oxford or Cambridge in England. The middle-class people owned small farms. The lower-class people were the servants. Slaves were the lowest social class of all.

Women worked in the home. They taught their daughters how to cook, sew, make soap and candles, and run a household. Men taught sons hunting and fieldwork.

Since North Carolina was an English colony, the Church of England was the official church. But people of all faiths were welcome there. There were Quakers, Presbyterians (press-buh-TEER-e-unz), Baptists, and other religious groups in the colony.

The colonists did not work all the time. They celebrated holidays and other festive occasions. Colonists liked to dance and listen to fiddle and bagpipe music. Men gathered at inns to visit and trade news. They also played games and raced horses.

A woman gathers butter from a churn.

Making a Living

Farming was an important part of North Carolina Colony's **economy**. In the coastal plain, colonists easily cleared the land and built many large plantations. The **piedmont** area was rocky and forested. So colonists built small farms there.

Farmers raised animals. They took cattle, hogs, sheep, and chickens to market. They grew peas, squash, corn, and wheat. They also grew tobacco and cotton.

Tobacco and cotton crops required many workers. After 1715, many farmers used slaves to tend their crops. Slavery was legal in North Carolina until the Thirteenth **Amendment** passed in 1865.

The colonists traded with the New England colonies, the Dutch West Indies, and England. They exported extra grains. They traded manufactured products such as tar, **pitch**, and **turpentine**. They also sold wood products such as shingles, planks, and barrels.

In the piedmont region, there were many swift rivers and streams. The colonists built mills along the waterways. The mills ground grain and later produced **textiles**.

A turpentine distillery in the North Carolina Colony

Food

North Carolina colonists ate beans, squash, and corn. Most families grew small gardens of potatoes, onions, rhubarb, and lettuce. Plantations often grew orchards of apples, peaches, and pears as well. Colonists also raised livestock, so they enjoyed beef, pork, mutton, and chicken.

The forest and the sea provided foods for the colonists, too. Walnuts, pecans, and maple syrup were all delicious treats. Wild game such as rabbit, turkey, and squirrel was plentiful. Because North Carolina is so close to the sea, the colonists ate much seafood. They ate cod, mackerel, and oysters.

The colonists grew or raised most of their own food. But wealthy colonists bought items like chocolate, coffee, sugar, and tea. Other colonists ate these on special occasions.

The water in North Carolina often made people sick. So North Carolinians made their own cider and brandy. They also drank milk when it was available.

Women cooked each meal in their homes' large fireplace. They used iron or brass pots and pans. Colonists ate from wooden plates and bowls.

A woman peels apples for an apple pie.

19

Clothing

Early colonists had to buy their clothes from England. Later, only wealthy colonists bought their clothes. They bought clothes made of velvet, lace, and silk.

In time, farmers grew flax and raised sheep. Flax is a plant with silklike fibers. Women spun flax fibers or sheep's wool into thread. Then they wove the thread into cloth.

The women dyed the cloth different colors using plants and berries. Then they cut the cloth and sewed clothes for their families.

Women and girls wore long dresses, aprons, and shawls. Men wore linen shirts and **doublets**. They also wore short, fitted pants called breeches, and kneesocks. All children wore dresses until they could walk. Then they wore the same types of clothing as adults.

Colonists also tanned leather to make coats, breeches, and shoes. Men who lived in the back country of North Carolina often wore deerskin breeches and **tunics**.

Some women wove extra fabric to sell for money.

Colonial Homes

People came from many different countries to live in the North Carolina Colony. There were people from Scotland, Ireland, Germany, and England. They all built different types of houses.

Some colonists built log houses. Others used wood and brick. To protect themselves from Native Americans, many early colonists built blockhouses or forts.

Most colonists built square or rectangular one-room houses. As their families grew, they added rooms. In log homes, colonists used clay to fill the gaps between logs. The small windows were covered with shutters. Few colonists could afford glass for their windows.

Most one-room homes had one large fireplace. The colonists used it for lighting, heating, and cooking.

Wealthy colonists built houses that were two stories tall. They had many rooms on each level. Each room had its own fireplace. These homes also had many separate buildings. They were used for different tasks, like cooking or washing laundry.

A woman draws water outside her log cabin.

Children

Tutors taught upper-class children in the North Carolina Colony. The lessons took place in the student's home. The tutors were almost a part of the family. They often lived on the family plantation.

After tutoring, a few boys attended college in England. Some went to American colleges such as Harvard, Yale, or William and Mary.

Most children in North Carolina worked on farms. Their parents needed their help and could not often afford education. For many years, North Carolina did not have public schools.

Some children became **apprentices**. Boys learned to be farmers, blacksmiths, tailors, and weavers. Girls learned to weave, spin, cook, and sew.

Missionaries began schools in North Carolina. In 1709, Anglican Charles Griffin began North Carolina's first school. In 1764, the assembly authorized a school in New Bern. It received money from the government. It also

educated ten poor children for free. In 1766, Reverend
James Tate began Tate's School. It prepared young men
for college until the **American Revolution** started.

When children had free time, they played games like
hopscotch. They made toys out of corncobs or wood.
Boys liked to go fishing, and many girls liked to have
tea parties.

A young woman helps on the farm by milking a cow.

Native Americans

The first Europeans in the North Carolina Colony met many different Native American tribes. The three largest tribes were the Tuscarora, the Catawba, and the Cherokee.

The Tuscarora grew angry as the colonists took their land. In 1711, they began to fight against colonists in the Tuscarora War. The Catawba fought with the colonists against the Tuscarora. By 1715, the Tuscarora had lost their land and moved north.

The Cherokee and the colonists got along for many years. The seven Cherokee clans grew corn, beans, and squash. They also hunted and gathered. The Cherokee had two governments. The White government ruled in times of peace. The Red government ruled in times of war.

In 1754, the French began to fight with the English for America's land. The Native Americans sided with the French. This was called the French and Indian War.

Native Americans raided North Carolina's settlements. North Carolina sent men to fight in the war. In 1763, the colonists made a treaty with the Native Americans.

But the colonists did not stop taking the Native American land. In 1838, the government forced thousands of Cherokee to move to **reservations** in Oklahoma. This journey is called the Trail of Tears.

Pomelock, a palisaded Native American village

The Road to Statehood

As the North Carolina Colony grew, it became successful. England wanted to earn money from the colony. So the English government passed laws to tax the colonists.

The Navigation Acts only allowed North Carolina's tobacco to be transported on English ships. And it could only be sent to England. There, the English sold the tobacco to other European countries for a profit.

In 1765, England's **Parliament** passed the Stamp Act. It said that certain documents had to be taxed and stamped to be legal. The colonists did not want to pay these taxes.

To protest, the First Provincial Congress met in New Bern in 1774. There, colonists elected North Carolina's delegates to the **First Continental Congress**.

In the **American Revolution**, North Carolina furnished many soldiers. On February 27, 1776, the colonists defeated the English at the Battle of Moore's Creek Bridge. In December 1776, North Carolina's Provincial Congress met. It adopted a state **constitution**.

The English won the Battle of Guilford Courthouse on March 15, 1781. From there, the English marched to Yorktown, Virginia, where they were soundly defeated. On November 21, 1789, North Carolina **ratified** the U.S. **Constitution**. It became the twelfth state of the new nation.

Today, North Carolina continues to be a leader in U.S. agriculture. And many people visit the same beaches and mountains that the colonists discovered.

Colonial soldiers fighting at the Battle of Guilford Courthouse

TIMELINE

1524 - Giovanni da Verrazzano sails past North Carolina's land

1526 - Lucas Vásques de Ayllón starts a North Carolina colony; it fails

1540 - Hernando de Soto explores North Carolina

1562 - France starts a colony in North Carolina; it fails

1585 - Sir Walter Raleigh starts a colony on Roanoke Island; it fails

1587 - Sir Walter Raleigh sends more colonists to Roanoke; they disappear

1629 - King Charles I grants North Carolina to Robert Heath

1650s - Colonists begin to move into North Carolina from other colonies

1662 - Virginia Colony names a commander to North Carolina area

1663 - King Charles II grants North Carolina's land to eight men

1664 - William Drummond becomes the first governor of Albemarle County

1691 - Proprietors name Philip Ludwell governor for all of Carolina

1709 - Charles Griffin begins North Carolina's first school

1711 - Tuscarora War begins; ends four years later

1712 - Carolina Colony is divided into North Carolina and South Carolina

1715 - Law passes giving North Carolina towns representation in assembly

1722 - Edenton becomes the seat of North Carolina's government

1729 - North Carolina becomes a royal colony

1754 - French and Indian War begins

1763 - Colonists form treaty with the Native Americans to end French and Indian War

1765 - Parliament passes the Stamp Act

1776 - Battle of Moore's Creek Bridge; North Carolina Colony adopts state constitution

1781 - Battle of Guilford Courthouse

1789 - North Carolina approves the U.S. Constitution

Glossary

Amendment - a change to the constitution of the United States.

American Revolution - 1775-1783. A war between England and its colonies in America. The colonists won their independence and created the United States.

apprentice - a person who learns a trade or craft from a skilled worker.

charter - a written contract that states a colony's boundaries and form of government.

constitution - the laws that govern a state or country.

doublet - a close-fitting jacket worn by men.

economy - the way a colony uses its money, goods, and natural resources.

First Continental Congress - 1774. A meeting of delegates from all of the colonies, except Georgia, to discuss problems with England's rule over the colonies.

freeman - a man free from bondage or slavery. A freeman often owned land and had the right to vote for assembly members.

militia - a group of citizens trained for war and other emergencies.

missionary - a person who spreads a church's religion.

Parliament - England's lawmaking group.

piedmont - land lying at the base of the mountains.

pitch - a black substance that comes from natural materials such as tar.

proprietor - one granted ownership of a colony, who is responsible for forming government and distributing land.

ratify - to officially approve.

reservation - land set aside by the government for Native Americans to live on.

surveyor - one who collects information about land.

textiles - of or having to do with the designing or manufacturing of cloth.

tunic - a long shirt, with or without sleeves, worn belted at the waist.

turpentine - a substance obtained from pine and fir trees.

Web Sites

North Carolina Encyclopedia http://statelibrary.dcr.state.nc.us/nc/cover.htm
Look up fun facts about North Carolina with this online encyclopedia.

North Carolina's Historical People and Places http://www.itpi.dpi.state.nc.us/nchistorical
Learn about battle sites, first towns, and famous people in North Carolina.

These sites are subject to change. Go to your favorite search engine and type in North Carolina Colony for more sites.

Index